From Clicks to Clients:

Mastering PPC Lead Generation for Maximum Conversions

By Joel Erlichson

Table Of Contents

1. Introduction

Definition of PPC lead generation

PPC lead generation is a digital marketing strategy that involves using paid advertising campaigns to attract potential customers to a website or landing page and convert them into leads. PPC, which stands for pay-per-click, refers to the method of payment, where advertisers pay a fee for each click on their ads.

The main goal of PPC lead generation is to drive traffic to a website or landing page and encourage visitors to take a specific action, such as filling out a form, subscribing to a newsletter, or calling a phone number. This action is typically the first step in a longer customer journey that ultimately leads to a purchase or conversion.

Platforms that use PPC lead generation include search engines such as Google and Bing, social media platforms such as Facebook, LinkedIn, and Twitter, and other display networks. These platforms offer advertisers the ability to target specific demographics, interests, and behaviors, allowing them to reach the most relevant audience for their products or services.

To launch a successful PPC lead generation campaign, businesses must first identify their target audience and understand their needs and preferences. This includes selecting the right keywords and creating effective ad copy that resonates with their audience.

Once the ads are up and running, the success of the campaign depends on several factors, including the relevance and quality of the landing page, the targeting of the audience, and the effectiveness of the call-to-action.

One of the key benefits of PPC lead generation is the ability to measure and optimize campaigns in real-time. By tracking key metrics such as click-through rate, cost-per-click, and conversion rate, businesses can quickly identify what's working and what's not and make adjustments accordingly.

In addition to traditional PPC campaigns, businesses can also leverage advanced strategies such as retargeting, which involves showing ads to people who have already visited a website or engaged with a brand in some way, and lookalike targeting, which involves targeting people who have similar characteristics to an existing customer base.

Overall, PPC lead generation can be a highly effective way to drive targeted traffic and generate leads for a business. However, it requires a solid understanding of the audience and careful planning and execution to achieve success.

Why PPC lead generation is important

PPC lead generation is an important digital marketing strategy that can help businesses drive growth and revenue. In this article, we'll explore why PPC lead generation is important and how it can benefit businesses of all sizes.

1) Attracting High-Quality Leads

One of the primary benefits of PPC lead generation is that it allows businesses to attract high-quality leads who are actively searching for products or services related to their business. By using targeted keywords and ad copy, businesses can ensure that their ads are being seen by people who are most likely to be interested in what they have to offer.

For example, if a business sells running shoes, they can create PPC ads that target keywords such as "running shoes," "athletic footwear," and "sneakers." This ensures that their ads are being seen by people who are actively searching for these types of products, increasing the likelihood that they will click on the ad and ultimately convert into a lead.

2) Predictable Costs

Another benefit of PPC lead generation is that it offers predictable costs. Unlike traditional advertising methods such as TV or print ads, PPC allows businesses to set a specific budget for their campaigns and only pay when someone clicks on their ad. This ensures that businesses are only paying for results, making it a more cost-effective way to generate leads.

3) Real-Time Optimization

PPC lead generation also allows businesses to optimize their campaigns in real-time. By tracking key metrics such as click-through rate, cost-per-click, and conversion rate, businesses can quickly identify what's working and what's not and make adjustments accordingly. This allows them to continually refine their campaigns and improve their results over time.

4) Increased Brand Visibility

PPC lead generation can also help businesses increase their brand visibility and awareness. By appearing at the top of search engine results pages and on popular social media platforms, businesses can increase their exposure to potential customers and establish themselves as a leader in their industry.

5) Targeted Advertising

Finally, PPC lead generation offers targeted advertising capabilities that are unmatched by traditional advertising methods. By using advanced targeting options such as geographic targeting, demographic targeting, and behavioral targeting, businesses can ensure that their ads are being seen by the most relevant audience for their products or services.

Overview of CalculatedLeads.com

CalculatedLeads.com is a digital marketing agency that specializes in PPC lead generation. Their PPC services are designed to help businesses attract high-quality leads and drive growth and revenue.

The team at CalculatedLeads.com begins by conducting a thorough analysis of a client's business and target audience to identify the most effective PPC strategies. This includes selecting the right keywords, creating compelling ad copy, and leveraging advanced targeting options to ensure that ads are being seen by the most relevant audience.

Once the PPC campaign is launched, CalculatedLeads.com closely monitors the performance of the ads, tracking key metrics such as click-through rate, cost-per-click, and conversion rate. They use this data to optimize the campaign in real-time, making adjustments to maximize results and ensure that the client is getting the most out of their advertising budget.

In addition to traditional PPC campaigns, CalculatedLeads.com also offers advanced PPC strategies such as retargeting and lookalike targeting. Retargeting involves showing ads to people who have already visited a client's website or engaged with their brand in some way. Lookalike targeting involves targeting people who have similar characteristics to an existing customer base.

Overall, CalculatedLeads.com's PPC services are designed to help businesses achieve their growth and revenue goals by attracting high-quality leads and driving conversions. With their expertise in PPC lead generation and advanced targeting capabilities, CalculatedLeads.com is a valuable partner for businesses looking to leverage the power of PPC advertising.

2. Setting Up Your PPC Campaign

Choosing the right keywords

Pay-per-click (PPC) advertising is one of the most popular forms of digital marketing, and it can be an effective way to reach your target audience and drive traffic to your website. However, to get the most out of your PPC campaign, you need to choose the right keywords. In this article, we'll provide some tips for selecting the right keywords for your PPC campaign.

1) Understand Your Audience

The first step in selecting the right keywords for your PPC campaign is to understand your audience. Who are they, what are their interests, and what are their pain points? Once you have a clear understanding of your target audience, you can start to identify the keywords that they are likely to search for when they are looking for products or services like yours.

2. Conduct Keyword Research

The next step is to conduct keyword research. There are many tools available that can help you find the right keywords for your PPC campaign, including Google Keyword Planner, SEMrush, and Ahrefs. These tools can give you insights into the volume of searches for specific keywords, as well as the level of competition for those keywords.

When conducting keyword research, it's important to focus on long-tail keywords. These are keywords that are more specific and targeted than general keywords, and they tend to have less competition. For example, instead of targeting the keyword "shoes," you might target the long-tail keyword "women's running shoes."

3. Focus on Relevant Keywords

When selecting keywords for your PPC campaign, it's important to focus on keywords that are relevant to your business. You don't want to waste money on clicks from people who are not interested in your products or services. To ensure that your keywords are relevant, consider the intent behind the search. For example, if someone searches for "best running shoes for women," they are likely to be interested in purchasing running shoes, so this would be a relevant keyword for a shoe retailer.

4. Analyze Your Competitors

Analyzing your competitors' keywords can be a great way to find new keyword opportunities for your PPC campaign. Look at the keywords that your competitors are bidding on, as well as the ad copy they are using. This can give you ideas for new keywords to target, as well as insights into how to craft your ad copy to stand out from the competition.

5. Continuously Optimize Your Campaign

Finally, it's important to continuously optimize your PPC campaign based on the performance of your keywords. Monitor your campaigns regularly and adjust your keyword targeting as needed. This can help you to maximize the effectiveness of your campaign and ensure that you are getting the best return on your investment.

In conclusion, choosing the right keywords for your PPC campaign is essential for reaching your target audience and driving traffic to your website. By understanding your audience, conducting keyword research, focusing on relevant keywords, analyzing your competitors, and continuously optimizing your campaign, you can create a successful PPC campaign that drives results for your business.

Writing Effective Ad Copy

Pay-per-click (PPC) advertising can be an incredibly effective way to generate leads for your business. However, to get the most out of your PPC campaigns, you need to write effective ad copy that grabs the attention of your target audience and convinces them to click through to your website. In this article, we'll provide some tips for writing effective ad copy for PPC leads.

1. Focus on Benefits

When writing ad copy for your PPC campaign, it's important to focus on the benefits of your product or service. Don't just list the features; explain how those features will benefit your target audience. For example, if you are selling a fitness program, don't just say "lose weight"; say "lose weight and feel more confident in your own skin."

2. Use Emotive Language

Emotive language can be incredibly powerful in ad copy. Use words that evoke emotions and feelings in your target audience, such as "exciting," "life-changing," or "unforgettable." However, make sure to use emotive language in a way that is authentic and relevant to your product or service.

3. Be Specific

Being specific in your ad copy can help you stand out from the competition and grab the attention of your target audience. Use specific numbers, statistics, or examples to illustrate the benefits of your product or service. For example, instead of saying "get more leads," say "increase your leads by 50% in just one month."

4. Speak to Your Target Audience

Make sure your ad copy speaks directly to your target audience. Use language and tone that resonates with them and addresses their specific pain points or challenges. Consider creating different ad variations that speak to different segments of your target audience.

5. Include a Clear Call to Action

Your ad copy should always include a clear call to action (CTA) that tells your target audience what you want them to do next. Use action-oriented language, such as "sign up now," "register today," or "learn more." Make sure your CTA is clear and easy to follow.

6. Test and Optimize

Finally, it's important to test and optimize your ad copy regularly. Create multiple variations of your ad copy and test them against each other to see which performs best. Make changes and adjustments based on the results, and continue to optimize your ad copy over time.

In conclusion, writing effective ad copy for PPC leads requires a combination of creativity, clarity, and specificity. By focusing on the benefits, using emotive language, being specific, speaking to your target audience, including a clear call to action, and testing and optimizing your ad copy, you can create PPC campaigns that generate leads and drive results for your business.

Selecting the Right Landing Page

When it comes to pay-per-click (PPC) advertising, selecting the right landing page is just as important as selecting the right keywords and ad copy. Your landing page is where your potential customers will be directed after clicking on your ad, and it can make or break the success of your PPC campaign. In this article, we'll explore some tips for selecting the right landing page for your PPC leads.

1. Match Your Landing Page to Your Ad

The landing page you choose should be directly relevant to the ad your potential customers clicked on. If your ad is promoting a specific product or service, the landing page should provide more information about that product or service. Make sure the language, imagery, and messaging on your landing page are consistent with your ad copy to create a seamless user experience.

2. Keep it Simple

Your landing page should be easy to navigate and understand. Avoid cluttered or complicated layouts, and make sure the most important information is prominently displayed. Use clear and concise language to convey your message and make it easy for potential customers to take the desired action, such as filling out a form or making a purchase.

3. Be Mobile-Friendly

With more and more people accessing the internet on their mobile devices, it's crucial that your landing page is mobile-friendly. Make sure your landing page is optimized for mobile devices, with a responsive design that adjusts to fit different screen sizes. Test your landing page on multiple devices to ensure a positive user experience for all potential customers.

4. Focus on User Experience

When choosing a landing page for your PPC campaign, put yourself in the shoes of your potential customers. What information are they looking for? What action do you want them to take? Make sure your landing page provides a positive user experience by providing the information they need and making it easy for them to take the desired action.

5. Measure and Optimize

Finally, it's important to measure and optimize your landing page regularly. Track your landing page's performance, including bounce rates, time on page, and conversion rates, and make changes based on the data. A/B testing can be a useful tool for testing different landing page variations to see which performs best.

In conclusion, selecting the right landing page for your PPC leads requires careful consideration and attention to detail. By matching your landing page to your ad, keeping it simple, being mobile-friendly, focusing on user experience, and measuring and optimizing your landing page, you can create a successful PPC campaign that drives results for your business.

Creating Compelling Calls-To-Action

As a business owner, you want your website visitors to take action, whether it's to make a purchase, sign up for a newsletter, or request more information. That's where calls-to-action (CTAs) come in. A CTA is a message that encourages your visitors to take a specific action on your website. The effectiveness of your CTA can have a huge impact on your conversion rates. In this article, we'll explore some tips for creating compelling calls-to-action.

1. Make it Clear and Specific

Your CTA should be clear and specific about what action you want your visitors to take. Use action-oriented language, such as "buy now," "register today," or "download our free guide." Make sure your CTA is prominently displayed and stands out visually on your website.

2. Create a Sense of Urgency

Creating a sense of urgency can be a powerful motivator for your visitors to take action. Use language that implies a limited-time offer, such as "limited time only," "while supplies last," or "act now." You can also use a countdown timer to create a sense of urgency.

3. Use Social Proof

Social proof is the idea that people are more likely to take action if they see others doing the same thing. Use social proof in your CTA by including testimonials or reviews from satisfied customers. You can also use numbers or statistics to demonstrate the popularity or effectiveness of your product or service.

4. Offer Incentives

Offering incentives can be a great way to encourage your visitors to take action. Offer a free trial, discount, or bonus for taking the desired action. Make sure your incentive is relevant to your product or service and provides real value to your visitors.

5. Test and Optimize

Finally, it's important to test and optimize your CTAs regularly. Try different variations of your CTA to see which performs best. Test different colors, wording, placement, and design. Use A/B testing to compare different versions of your CTA and make data-driven decisions about which one to use.

In conclusion, creating compelling calls-to-action is essential for driving conversions on your website. By making your CTA clear and specific, creating a sense of urgency, using social proof, offering incentives, and testing and optimizing your CTA, you can encourage your visitors to take action and drive results for your business.

3. Optimizing Your PPC Campaign

Understanding Your Metrics

When running a PPC campaign, understanding your metrics is critical for optimizing your campaign and getting the most out of your investment. By tracking and analyzing your campaign data, you can identify areas for improvement and make data-driven decisions to drive better results. In this article, we'll take a deep dive into some of the key metrics you should be tracking for your PPC campaign.

Click-through rate (CTR) is the percentage of people who click on your ad after seeing it. A high CTR indicates that your ad is compelling and relevant to your target audience. A low CTR, on the other hand, can indicate that your ad needs improvement or that your targeting needs to be refined. To improve your CTR, consider testing different ad copy, targeting options, and keywords.

Conversion rate is the percentage of people who take a desired action on your website, such as making a purchase or filling out a form, after clicking on your ad. A high conversion rate indicates that your landing page and overall user experience are effective at converting visitors into customers. To improve your conversion rate, consider testing different landing pages, offers, and calls-to-action.

Cost per click (CPC) is the amount you pay each time someone clicks on your ad. CPC can vary based on competition for keywords and targeting options. To get the most out of your budget, focus on targeting high-intent keywords and refining your targeting to reach the right audience.

Quality score is a metric used by Google Ads to measure the relevance and quality of your ad and landing page. A high quality score can lead to lower CPCs and better ad placement. To improve your quality score, focus on creating relevant ad copy, targeting high-intent keywords, and creating a high-quality landing page experience.

Return on ad spend (ROAS) is a measure of the revenue generated from your PPC campaign compared to the amount you spend on advertising. A high ROAS indicates that your campaign is generating a positive return on investment. To improve your ROAS, focus on optimizing your conversion rate, targeting high-intent keywords, and refining your targeting to reach the right audience.

In conclusion, understanding your metrics is essential for optimizing your PPC campaign and driving better results. By tracking and analyzing your CTR, conversion rate, CPC, quality score, and ROAS, you can identify areas for improvement and make data-driven decisions to improve your campaign performance.

Split Testing your Ads and Landing Pages

Split testing, also known as A/B testing, is a powerful technique used to optimize your PPC campaigns. By creating multiple versions of your ads and landing pages and testing them against each other, you can identify which versions perform better and make data-driven decisions to improve your campaign performance. In this article, we'll explore the benefits of split testing and share some best practices to help you get the most out of your testing.

Why split test your ads and landing pages?

1. Improve performance: Split testing allows you to identify which ad or landing page variation generates the highest click-through rates, conversion rates, and ultimately, ROI.
2. Reduce risk: By testing multiple variations, you reduce the risk of relying on a single version that may not be as effective as others.
3. Refine your messaging: Split testing can help you fine-tune your messaging to better resonate with your target audience.
4. Stay competitive: By continually testing and optimizing your ads and landing pages, you can stay ahead of the competition and maintain a competitive edge.

Best practices for split testing your ads and landing pages

1. Define your goals: Before you start testing, define what you want to achieve with your campaign. Are you looking to increase conversions, click-through rates, or ROI? Having a clear goal in mind will help you make data-driven decisions and avoid aimless testing.
2. Test one variable at a time: To accurately measure the impact of each variation, only test one variable at a time. This could be the ad copy, the landing page headline, or the call-to-action button. By testing one variable at a time, you can determine which specific change had the greatest impact on performance.
3. Test a significant sample size: To ensure the results of your test are statistically significant, you need to test each variation on a large enough sample size. If your sample size is too small, your results may not be reliable.
4. Monitor your results: Keep a close eye on your test results and analyze them regularly. Don't be afraid to pause or end a test if the results are clear enough to make a decision.
5. Take action: Once you've identified the winning variation, take action and implement the changes in your campaign. Remember to continue testing and optimizing to ensure you're always improving.

Adjusting your Bids

Adjusting your bids is an essential part of optimizing your PPC campaigns for better performance. Bid adjustments can help you ensure that your ads are showing to the right audience and at the right time, which can ultimately improve your click-through rates, conversion rates, and ROI. In this article, we'll discuss why bid adjustments are important and share some best practices to help you get the most out of your ad spend.

Why adjust your bids?

1. Optimize ad position: Adjusting your bids can help you optimize your ad position on the search engine results page. By bidding higher, you can increase your chances of appearing at the top of the page, which can lead to more clicks and conversions.
2. Target specific audiences: Bid adjustments allow you to target specific audiences based on their location, device, time of day, and other factors. For example, you may want to increase your bids for users who are located near your business or for users who are searching on mobile devices.

3. Test and refine: Don't be afraid to test different bid adjustments and refine your strategy based on your results. By continually testing and optimizing, you can improve your ad performance and get the most out of your ad spend.

Best practices for adjusting your bids

1. Set a budget: Before you start adjusting your bids, it's important to set a budget for your campaign. This will help you ensure that you're not overspending on your ads and that you're getting the most out of your ad spend.
2. Analyze your data: Regularly analyze your campaign data to identify trends and areas for improvement. Look at your click-through rates, conversion rates, and cost per conversion to determine which keywords and audiences are performing the best.
3. Start with small adjustments: When making bid adjustments, start with small changes to see how they affect your campaign performance. Gradually increase or decrease your bids based on your results.
4. Test and refine: Don't be afraid to test different bid adjustments and refine your strategy based on your results. By continually testing and optimizing, you can improve your ad performance and get the most out of your ad spend.

Conclusion

Adjusting your bids is an important part of optimizing your PPC campaigns for better performance. By targeting specific audiences, optimizing your ad position, and improving ad relevance, you can improve your click-through rates, conversion rates, and ROI. Remember to set a budget, analyze your data, start with small adjustments, and continually test and refine your strategy to get the most out of your ad spend.

Targeting your Audience Effectively

One of the biggest advantages of PPC advertising is the ability to target your audience with precision. By showing your ads only to those who are most likely to be interested in your product or service, you can increase the effectiveness of your campaigns and reduce wasted ad spend. In this article, we'll explore some strategies for targeting your audience effectively with PPC leads.

Most PPC advertising platforms offer a range of audience targeting options, including demographic, geographic, and interest-based targeting. By using these options, you can ensure that your ads are seen by the right people. For example, if you're selling luxury goods, you might target your ads to high-income earners or people in affluent areas.

Custom audiences allow you to target people who have already interacted with your brand in some way, such as by visiting your website or signing up for your email list. These audiences can be highly effective, as they have already shown an interest in your brand. You can also create lookalike audiences based on your custom audiences, which can help you reach new people who are similar to your existing customers.

Keywords are a critical component of any PPC campaign, as they determine when and where your ads are shown. By choosing the right keywords, you can ensure that your ads are seen by people who are actively searching for what you have to offer. However, it's important to use keywords wisely and avoid targeting keywords that are too broad or too competitive.

Effective targeting requires ongoing testing and refinement. By monitoring the performance of your campaigns and adjusting your targeting as needed, you can ensure that your ads are being shown to the right people. Use A/B testing to compare different targeting options and measure the impact on your conversion rates and ROI.

Finally, it's important to focus on relevance when targeting your audience with PPC leads. Your ads should be highly relevant to the people who are seeing them, with a clear message and a compelling offer. By focusing on relevance, you can increase the effectiveness of your campaigns and drive more leads and sales.

In conclusion, targeting your audience effectively is key to the success of any PPC campaign. By using audience targeting options, custom audiences, keywords, testing, and relevance, you can increase the effectiveness of your campaigns and drive more leads and sales. Keep these strategies in mind as you plan and execute your PPC campaigns, and you'll be on your way to success.

4. Converting PPC Leads

Nurturing Leads Through Email Marketing

When it comes to generating leads with PPC advertising, it's not enough to simply get people to click on your ads. To make the most of your investment, you need to nurture those leads and turn them into paying customers. One of the most effective ways to do this is through email marketing. In this article, we'll explore some strategies for nurturing your PPC leads with email marketing.

Send a welcome email

When someone signs up for your email list after clicking on your PPC ad, it's important to send a welcome email to introduce yourself and set expectations for what they can expect from your emails. This is an opportunity to provide additional value and start building a relationship with your new lead.

Segment your list

To make your email marketing more effective, it's important to segment your list based on the actions that people take after clicking on your PPC ad. For example, if someone clicks on an ad for a specific product or service, you can send them emails related to that product or service. This can help increase the relevance of your emails and make them more likely to be opened and clicked.

Provide value

The key to effective email marketing is providing value to your subscribers. This can take many forms, such as helpful tips, educational content, exclusive offers, and more. By providing value, you can build trust with your subscribers and keep them engaged with your brand.

Automate your emails

Automating your email marketing can help you save time and ensure that your subscribers receive the right message at the right time. For example, you might set up a series of automated emails that are triggered when someone signs up for your email list or makes a purchase.

Measure and refine

To make the most of your email marketing efforts, it's important to measure and refine your campaigns. Use analytics tools to track open rates, click-through rates, and other metrics, and adjust your campaigns as needed to improve performance.

In conclusion, email marketing is a powerful tool for nurturing your PPC leads and turning them into paying customers. By sending a welcome email, segmenting your list, providing value, automating your emails, and measuring and refining your campaigns, you can increase the effectiveness of your email marketing efforts and drive more sales. Keep these strategies in mind as you plan and execute your email marketing campaigns, and you'll be on your way to success.

Using Retargeting to Bring Leads Back

One of the biggest challenges in PPC advertising is converting leads into customers. Even if someone clicks on your ad and visits your website, they might not take the action you want them to, such as making a purchase or filling out a form. However, just because someone doesn't convert on their first visit doesn't mean they're lost forever. With retargeting, you can bring back lost PPC leads and turn them into paying customers. In this article, we'll explore some strategies for using retargeting to bring back lost PPC leads.

Set up retargeting campaigns

Retargeting allows you to show ads to people who have already visited your website but haven't converted. To set up a retargeting campaign, you'll need to install a retargeting pixel on your website that tracks visitors and adds them to a retargeting audience. Then, you can create ads that target this audience and encourage them to return to your website and complete the desired action.

Create personalized ads

To make your retargeting ads more effective, it's important to create personalized ads that speak directly to the interests and needs of your target audience. Use the data you've collected from your PPC campaigns and website analytics to create ads that are tailored to each stage of the buyer's journey.

Offer incentives

To entice lost PPC leads to return to your website and complete the desired action, consider offering incentives such as discounts, free trials, or exclusive content. These incentives can help overcome any objections or hesitations that the lead may have had on their first visit.

Use dynamic retargeting

Dynamic retargeting allows you to show ads that are personalized to the specific products or services that a lead viewed on your website. This can be a powerful way to bring back lost leads and encourage them to make a purchase.

Test and optimize

As with any PPC campaign, it's important to test and optimize your retargeting campaigns to ensure that you're getting the best possible results. Use analytics tools to track your ad performance and adjust your campaigns as needed to improve performance.

In conclusion, retargeting is a powerful tool for bringing back lost PPC leads and turning them into paying customers. By setting up retargeting campaigns, creating personalized ads, offering incentives, using dynamic retargeting, and testing and optimizing your campaigns, you can increase the effectiveness of your retargeting efforts and drive more sales. Keep these strategies in mind as you plan and execute your retargeting campaigns, and you'll be on your way to success.

Optimizing your Lead Capture Forms

PPC campaigns are an excellent way to generate leads for your business. However, getting clicks on your ads is just the first step. You need to have an effective lead capture form that converts those clicks into actual leads. In this article, we'll discuss some tips for optimizing your lead capture forms for PPC leads.

Keep it simple

One of the most important things to remember when creating your lead capture form is to keep it simple. Your form should only ask for essential information such as name, email address, and phone number. Too many fields can be overwhelming and may deter potential leads from filling out the form.

Make it visually appealing

The design of your lead capture form is also crucial in converting leads. Use contrasting colors for the background and form fields to make it visually appealing. The font should be easy to read, and the form should be optimized for mobile devices.

Provide context

When asking for information on your lead capture form, provide context for why you need it. For example, if you're asking for a phone number, explain that it's so you can follow up with the lead and provide them with more information about your product or service.

Use a strong call-to-action

Your lead capture form should have a clear and compelling call-to-action (CTA). Use action-oriented words such as "download," "subscribe," or "register" to encourage users to fill out the form. The CTA should be prominent and stand out on the page.

Test and refine

Like any aspect of your PPC campaign, it's essential to test and refine your lead capture form. Use A/B testing to try out different form designs, CTAs, and form lengths. Analyze the results to determine which version is the most effective in converting leads.

Consider using chatbots

Chatbots can be an effective way to capture leads as they allow for a more conversational approach. They can also help pre-qualify leads before they fill out a form, ensuring that you're only receiving high-quality leads.

In conclusion, optimizing your lead capture form is an essential step in converting PPC clicks into actual leads. By keeping your form simple, visually appealing, providing context, using a strong call-to-action, testing and refining, and considering the use of chatbots, you can improve the effectiveness of your lead capture form and ultimately drive more conversions for your business.

Building Trust with your Prospects

PPC campaigns are a great way to attract potential customers to your website. However, the journey from being a prospect to becoming a paying customer is not always straightforward. Trust is a crucial factor in building relationships with prospects, and this is especially true for those who discover your business through PPC leads. In this article, we'll discuss some effective ways to build trust with your prospects and turn them into loyal customers.

Provide value through content

Creating high-quality, informative content is an excellent way to establish your authority and expertise in your industry. Your content should be relevant to your target audience and address their pain points. By providing valuable information, you can position yourself as a thought leader and build trust with your prospects.

Use social proof

Social proof is a powerful tool in building trust with your prospects. You can use customer testimonials, case studies, and reviews to demonstrate that your business delivers on its promises. Share success stories of customers who have used your products or services and the positive outcomes they've experienced.

Respond to inquiries promptly

Promptly responding to inquiries from your prospects shows that you value their time and are committed to providing excellent customer service. Ensure that your website has a clear contact form or phone number, and make sure that inquiries are responded to in a timely manner. This can help establish a positive first impression and build trust with your prospects.

Personalize your communications

Personalizing your communications with prospects can help to establish a connection and build trust. Use their name and address their specific needs or concerns. Personalization can also extend to the design of your landing pages and the content of your emails.

Offer guarantees

Offering guarantees such as money-back guarantees, free trials, or warranties can be an effective way to build trust with your prospects. These guarantees show that you're confident in your products or services and are willing to stand behind them.

Provide exceptional customer service

Providing exceptional customer service is crucial in building trust with your prospects. Respond to questions and concerns promptly and go above and beyond to address their needs. By providing an outstanding customer experience, you can build a strong foundation of trust with your prospects.

In conclusion, building trust with your prospects is essential in converting them into loyal customers. By providing value through content, using social proof, responding to inquiries promptly, personalizing your communications, offering guarantees, and providing exceptional customer service, you can establish a strong foundation of trust with your prospects and turn them into loyal customers. Remember, trust is earned, not given, so it's essential to be consistent in your efforts to build and maintain trust with your prospects.

5. Advanced PPC Lead Generation Strategies

Using Lookalike Audiences to Find Similar Prospects

PPC advertising is a powerful tool for finding new customers and growing your business. However, targeting the right audience is crucial to the success of your campaigns. One way to expand your reach and find new customers is through lookalike audiences. In this article, we'll discuss what lookalike audiences are and how to use them to find similar prospects in PPC.

What are Lookalike Audiences?

Lookalike audiences are groups of people who share similar characteristics to your existing customers. These audiences are created using data from your existing customers, such as their demographics, interests, and behaviors. The platform then uses this data to find other people who share these same characteristics and who are likely to be interested in your business.

How to Use Lookalike Audiences in PPC

Upload Your Customer List

The first step in creating a lookalike audience is to upload a list of your existing customers to the advertising platform you're using. This list can include email addresses, phone numbers, or other identifying information. The platform will then use this data to find people who share similar characteristics.

Define Your Targeting

Once you've uploaded your customer list, you can define your targeting options. This can include factors such as location, age, interests, and behaviors. You can also specify the size of your lookalike audience.

Monitor Your Results

As with any PPC campaign, it's essential to monitor your results and make adjustments as needed. Keep an eye on your click-through rates, conversion rates, and other metrics to ensure that your campaign is performing well. You may need to make adjustments to your targeting options or your ad copy to optimize your results.

Benefits of Using Lookalike Audiences in PPC

Expand Your Reach

Lookalike audiences allow you to expand your reach and find new customers who are likely to be interested in your business. By targeting people who share similar characteristics to your existing customers, you can reach a broader audience and increase your chances of success.

Improve Your Conversion Rates

Because lookalike audiences are made up of people who are similar to your existing customers, they're more likely to be interested in your business and more likely to convert. This can help to improve your conversion rates and drive more sales.

Save Time and Money

Using lookalike audiences can save you time and money by targeting people who are more likely to be interested in your business. This can help to reduce your overall ad spend and improve your ROI.

In conclusion, using lookalike audiences is an effective way to find similar prospects in PPC advertising. By uploading your customer list and defining your targeting options, you can expand your reach, improve your conversion rates, and save time and money. Keep in mind that monitoring your results and making adjustments as needed is crucial to the success of your campaign. With the right approach, lookalike audiences can be a powerful tool in your PPC advertising arsenal.

Leveraging Social Media Ads for Lead Gen

Social media has become an integral part of our lives, and businesses have found that it can be a powerful tool for lead generation. However, simply running ads on social media platforms may not be enough to generate the leads you're looking for. In this article, we'll explore a unique approach to leveraging social media ads for lead generation.

Understand Your Audience

The first step in any successful lead generation campaign is to understand your audience. This includes their demographics, interests, behaviors, and pain points. Use this information to create targeted ads that speak directly to your audience's needs and wants.

Create a Compelling Offer

Once you've identified your target audience, it's time to create a compelling offer. This can be a discount, a free trial, or a valuable piece of content that your audience will find useful. The key is to make your offer irresistible, so your audience is motivated to take action.

Create a Landing Page

When someone clicks on your social media ad, they should be directed to a landing page that's designed to convert them into a lead. Your landing page should be visually appealing, easy to navigate, and clearly communicate the value of your offer. Use persuasive copy and images to convince your audience to take the desired action.

Use Retargeting Ads

Retargeting ads are a powerful tool for lead generation because they allow you to target people who have already shown an interest in your business. For example, if someone clicked on your ad but didn't convert, you can retarget them with a new ad that offers a different incentive to take action.

Nurture Your Leads

Once you've generated leads from your social media ads, it's essential to nurture them. Use email marketing campaigns to continue to provide value to your leads and move them through the sales funnel. Provide them with additional content and offers that address their pain points and show them the benefits of your product or service.

Measure and Refine

Finally, it's important to measure the success of your social media lead generation campaign and refine your approach as needed. Use analytics to track your conversion rates, click-through rates, and other metrics. Identify areas where you can improve your campaign and make adjustments accordingly.

In conclusion, leveraging social media ads for lead generation requires a unique approach that goes beyond simply running ads on social media platforms. By understanding your audience, creating a compelling offer, using retargeting ads, nurturing your leads, and measuring and refining your approach, you can generate high-quality leads from social media ads and grow your business.

Using Google Display Network for Branding and Lead Gen

Google Display Network (GDN) is a powerful tool that allows businesses to reach potential customers by displaying ads across a network of websites. With access to over 2 million websites and 90% of internet users, GDN can be a valuable tool for both branding and lead generation. In this article, we'll explore the benefits of using GDN for both purposes and how to effectively utilize the platform.

Branding with GDN

One of the key benefits of using GDN for branding is the ability to reach a large audience quickly. With the ability to display ads on millions of websites, businesses can quickly increase brand awareness and reach potential customers who may not have otherwise been aware of their brand.

To effectively use GDN for branding, businesses should focus on creating visually appealing ads that showcase their brand and messaging. This can include using high-quality images or videos, clear and concise messaging, and consistent branding elements such as colors and logos. It's also important to use targeting options such as demographics, interests, and topics to ensure ads are being displayed to the right audience.

Lead Generation with GDN

While branding is an important aspect of any advertising campaign, businesses also need to generate leads to grow their customer base. GDN can be an effective tool for lead generation by reaching potential customers who may be interested in their products or services.

To use GDN for lead generation, businesses should focus on creating ads that offer value to potential customers, such as free resources or product trials. It's also important to use targeting options such as remarketing, in-market audiences, and affinity audiences to ensure ads are being displayed to users who are most likely to be interested in the offer.

In addition to creating valuable ads, businesses should also focus on optimizing their landing pages to increase the chances of conversion. This can include using clear and concise messaging, a strong call-to-action, and a simple and user-friendly layout.

Best Practices for GDN

To effectively use GDN for both branding and lead generation, businesses should keep in mind the following best practices:

- Use visually appealing ads that showcase your brand and messaging
- Use targeting options such as demographics, interests, and topics to ensure ads are being displayed to the right audience
- Focus on creating ads that offer value to potential customers
- Optimize landing pages to increase conversion rates
- Continuously monitor and adjust campaigns to ensure maximum effectiveness

In conclusion, Google Display Network can be a valuable tool for businesses looking to increase brand awareness and generate leads. By creating visually appealing ads that offer value to potential customers and using effective targeting options, businesses can effectively leverage GDN for both branding and lead generation.

Implementing Cross-Channel Marketing to Drive Leads

In today's digital age, businesses have access to a wide range of channels to reach potential customers. From social media to email marketing, there are many ways to connect with your target audience. However, implementing a cross-channel marketing strategy can be even more effective in driving leads and converting them into customers. In this article, we'll explore the benefits of cross-channel marketing and how to effectively implement it to drive leads.

Benefits of Cross-Channel Marketing

Cross-channel marketing allows businesses to reach potential customers through multiple channels, which can increase the chances of conversion. By having a consistent message across all channels, businesses can build brand awareness and trust with potential customers.

Additionally, cross-channel marketing can help businesses reach potential customers at different stages of the buying cycle. For example, a potential customer may first discover a business through social media, but then make the final decision to purchase after receiving an email or seeing a display ad.

Identifying Channels to Include in Cross-Channel Marketing

The first step in implementing a cross-channel marketing strategy is to identify the channels that will be included. This will depend on the target audience and the goals of the campaign. Some channels to consider include:

- Social media: Platforms such as Facebook, Instagram, and LinkedIn can be effective in reaching potential customers and driving leads.
- Email marketing: Email is a powerful tool for nurturing leads and converting them into customers.
- Display advertising: Display ads can be used to reach potential customers across the web, including on Google and social media.
- Video advertising: Video ads can be used on platforms such as YouTube and social media to engage potential customers and drive leads.

Creating a Consistent Message Across Channels

Once the channels have been identified, it's important to create a consistent message across all channels. This includes using consistent branding, messaging, and calls-to-action. By having a consistent message, businesses can build brand awareness and trust with potential customers.

Using Data to Optimize Cross-Channel Marketing

To effectively implement cross-channel marketing, businesses should use data to optimize their campaigns. This includes tracking metrics such as conversion rates, click-through rates, and engagement rates across all channels. By analyzing this data, businesses can make informed decisions about which channels to focus on and how to optimize their campaigns for maximum effectiveness.

Best Practices for Cross-Channel Marketing

To effectively implement cross-channel marketing, businesses should keep in mind the following best practices:

- Identify the channels that will be included in the campaign
- Create a consistent message across all channels
- Use data to optimize campaigns
- Test and refine campaigns over time to improve effectiveness

In conclusion, implementing a cross-channel marketing strategy can be an effective way to drive leads and convert them into customers. By identifying the channels to include, creating a consistent message, and using data to optimize campaigns, businesses can effectively leverage cross-channel marketing to reach potential customers and grow their customer base.

6. Conclusion

Final Thoughts

In conclusion, PPC lead generation is a critical component of any successful digital marketing campaign. As we've seen in this article, there are numerous strategies and tactics you can employ to optimize your PPC campaigns and generate more high-quality leads for your business.

First, it's important to start with a solid foundation by selecting the right keywords, writing effective ad copy, and choosing the most appropriate landing pages for your audience. These elements all work together to create a cohesive and compelling message that resonates with your target audience and encourages them to take action.

Once your campaigns are up and running, it's crucial to monitor and analyze your metrics to understand how your ads and landing pages are performing. Split testing is an essential tool for optimizing your campaigns and improving your ROI, allowing you to compare different ad and landing page variations to determine which ones are most effective.

Targeting your audience effectively is another critical aspect of successful PPC lead generation. By understanding your ideal customer personas and tailoring your campaigns to their unique needs and preferences, you can increase your chances of reaching the right people at the right time.

Converting your PPC leads into paying customers requires a strategic approach as well. By nurturing leads through email marketing, using retargeting to bring them back to your site, optimizing your lead capture forms, and building trust with your prospects, you can create a seamless and enjoyable customer experience that encourages them to make a purchase.

Finally, advanced PPC lead generation strategies like using lookalike audiences, leveraging social media ads, and implementing cross-channel marketing can take your campaigns to the next level, providing even more opportunities for growth and success.

In conclusion, there's no one-size-fits-all approach to PPC lead generation. It requires a combination of research, planning, testing, and ongoing optimization to achieve the best results. By staying up to date with the latest trends and technologies and continually refining your approach, you can create successful PPC campaigns that drive more high-quality leads and help your business grow and succeed.

www.ingramcontent.com/pod-product-compliance
Lightning Source LLC
Chambersburg PA
CBHW071143220526
45467CB00015B/1805